Luna Peak Publishing, Sierra Madre, California.
www.lunapeakpublishing.com

ISBN: 979-8-9861782-0-2
Printed and bound in the United States of America.

The Grief Workbook

For Kids

By Gracelyn Bateman & Melody Lomboy-Lowe

LUNA PEAK PUBLISHING

Hey friend!

grief is really tough. We want you to know that you are not alone. This workbook was created to help you work through your feelings after losing an important person in your life.

Take your time while filling out this workbook, and have fun. Remember, you are not alone in your grief.

From your fellow grief friends,
Gracelyn & Melody

About You

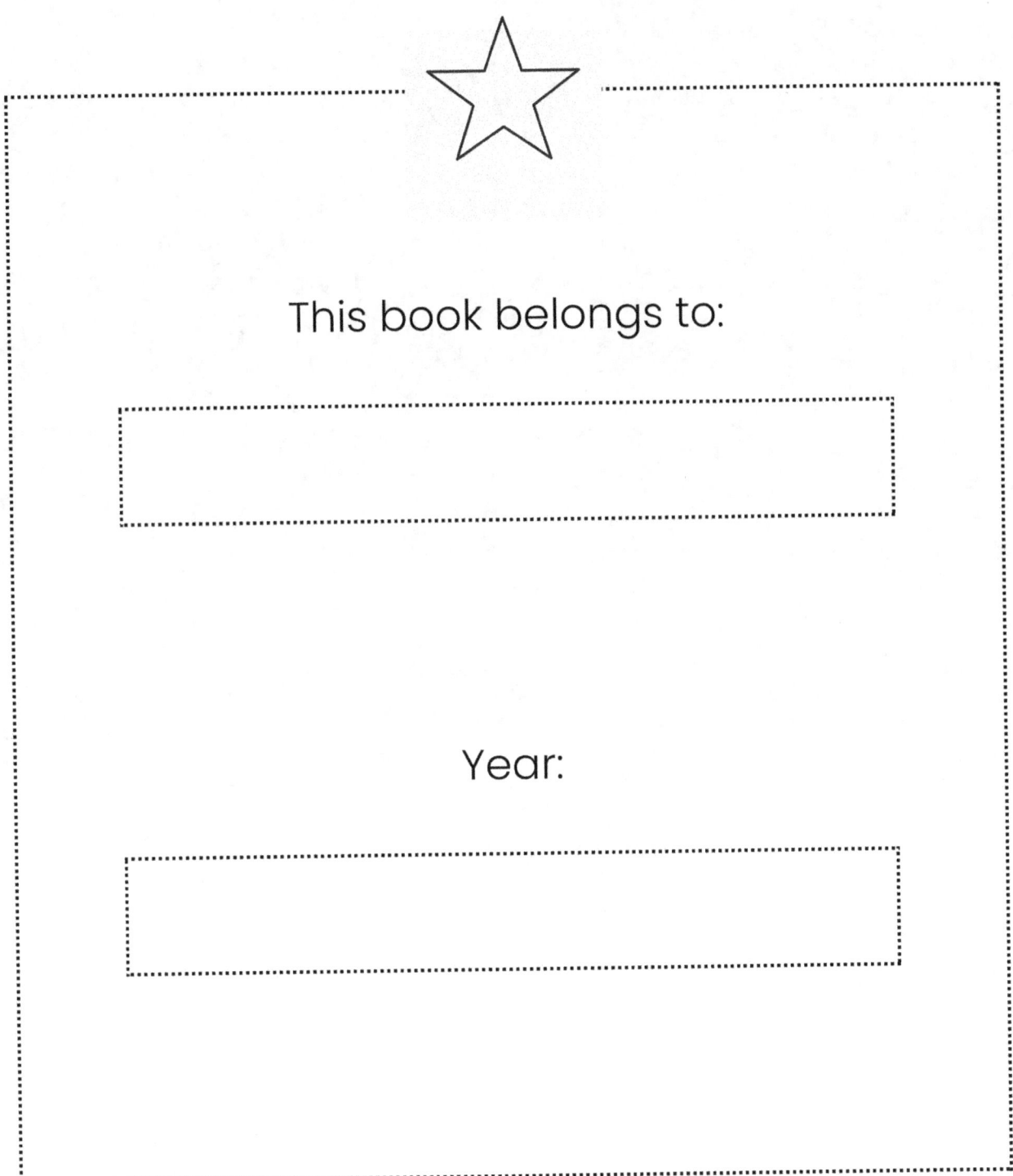

This book belongs to:

Year:

About Them

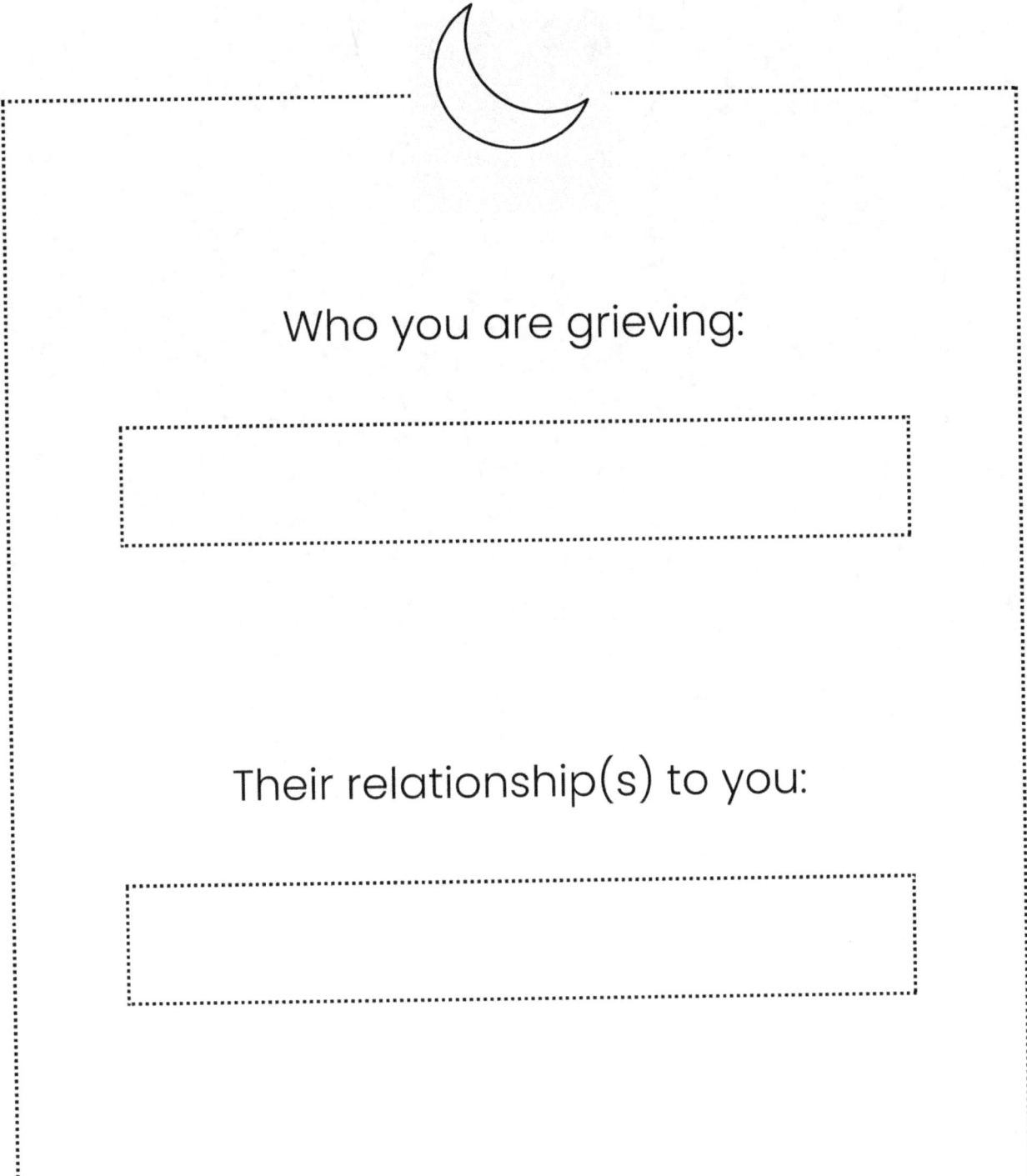

Who you are grieving:

Their relationship(s) to you:

You can use the blank
pages to write more or to
share about other losses

Let's Talk About Them
- PART 1 -

What were your loved one's favorite things?

Color:

Nickname:

Activity:

Food:

Drink:

Dessert:

What Were They Like?

Share about your loved one. What were they like?

_____

_____

_____

_____

_____

_____

_____

Crying Is Normal

It is normal and healthy to cry. Color in the locations where you have cried, and add more places in the empty tears.

Would You Rather
- PART 1 -

Color in what you like best.

Spend time alone	Spend time with others

or

Play outside	Play inside

or

Talk about your grief with others	Think about your grief by yourself

or

Stay home when you're feeling sad	Leave the house when you're feeling sad

or

Safe Zone

Where do you feel safe to express your emotions?

_____

_____

_____

_____

Why do these places feel safe for you?

_____

_____

_____

_____

Safe Hearts

Who makes you feel safe to
express your emotions?

What makes them feel safe to you?

What Is GRIEF?

Did you know what grief was before your loved one died?

Yes	No

What did you think grief would feel like?

_____

_____

_____

Floating Feelings

Sometimes grief can include many different feelings and emotions.
Color in the emotions you have felt, and add more.

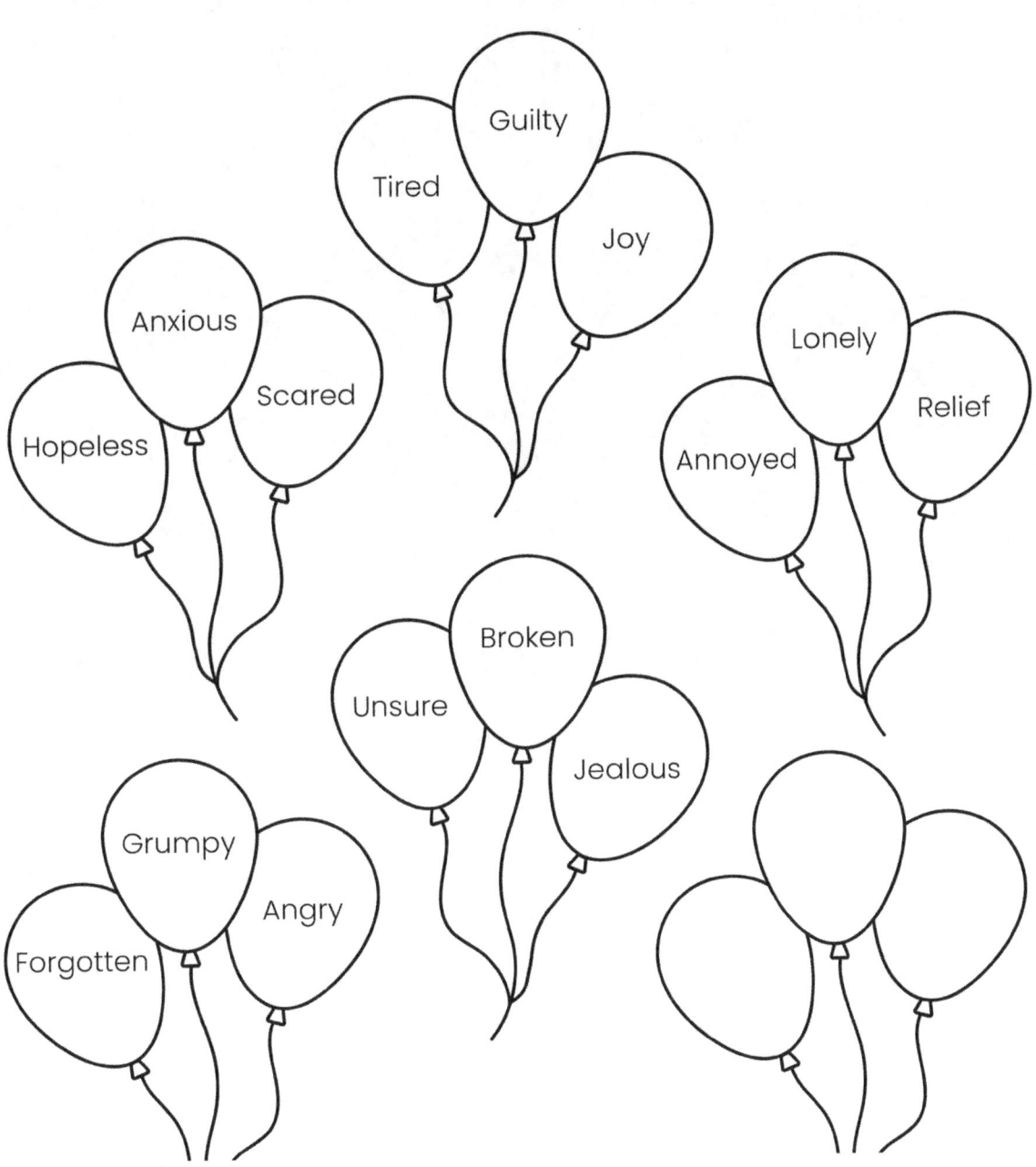

Comforting Words

Did anyone share comforting words with you?

_____

_____

_____

_____

How did it feel to hear those words?

_____

_____

_____

_____

Unhelpful Words

Did anyone say words that upset you?

How did you react?

On Tough Days

Who do you like to talk to, if you want to talk?

What is a place that brings you comfort?

What sounds or music do you like to listen to?

Would You Rather

- PART 2 -

Color in what you like best.

| Keep old traditions | or | Start new traditions |

| Celebrate their birthday and death anniversary | or | Treat their birthday and death anniversary as ordinary days |

| Listen to music | or | Have quiet time |

| Be serious | or | Laugh and joke |

The Grief Creature

If grief was a creature, how would you draw it?

Write Them a Letter

- Part 1 -

Lately I've been feeling:

A question I have for you:

A memory with you that makes me smile:

Play BINGO

Color in the experiences that happened to you before, during, and after the memorial services.

Someone asked you how your loved one died	It felt like people were staring at you	You hid from relatives	Snotty crying	You ran out of tissues
You bought new clothes for the services	You did not cry	You spoke at the funeral	You wanted everyone to leave	You heard a new story about your loved one
You met new people at the funeral	You forgot they died	FREE SPACE	You ate a lot of candy	You didn't feel like eating
You had trouble sleeping	You slept a lot	You don't like the smell of flowers now	You saw friends at the services	You were taken out for ice cream
You don't want to wear the funeral clothes again	People said "Sorry" to you	You received hugs	You skipped school for a few days	You asked a lot of questions

Memorial Events

What else happened at the memorial?

_____

_____

_____

_____

_____

_____

_____

Feel Good Things
- PART 1 -

What do you like to eat?

What do you like to drink?

Your Helpers

Have you been helped by friends and family?
List their names:

_____

_____

_____

How have they helped you?

_____

_____

_____

_____

Let's Talk About Them
- PART 2 -

What were your loved one's favorite things?

Place:

Team:

Saying:

Movie:

Show:

Plant:

Word Search
- PART 1 -

```
H P S Y W F L Z M F W T H M H
I E S H A F B A I R R M O Q E
K O L M A P M X I O T R N Z A
V N I P J R F K P C T J O K L
W L U B M X E P V J E P R A I
Y F J X M W U B N P W P N E N
H U R T M S Y A C D P R S E G
N O I T C E L F E R U C Z R B
G Y M M A Q Y G C O R C C A P
S K B J G I L M J X O Q P C W
C O M M U N I C A T E F J S A
W V X X A D F I B M L A I G W
```

SHARE   CARE   FAMILY   HONOR
HURT   JOURNAL   COMMUNICATE   REFLECTION
HEALING   SPECIAL   HELP   SUPPORT

Where Are They?

How would you describe where your
loved one is now?

_____

_____

_____

_____

_____

_____

Similar & Different

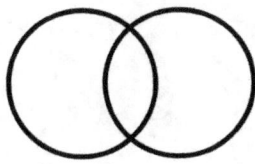

How are you similar to your loved one?

How are you different from your loved one?

Grief In Your Body

Circle where you feel
grief in your body.

How Does Grief Feel?

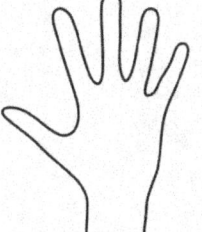

Describe how grief feels in your body.

Grief Emotions

Draw faces on the emojis below to show the emotions that you have been feeling.

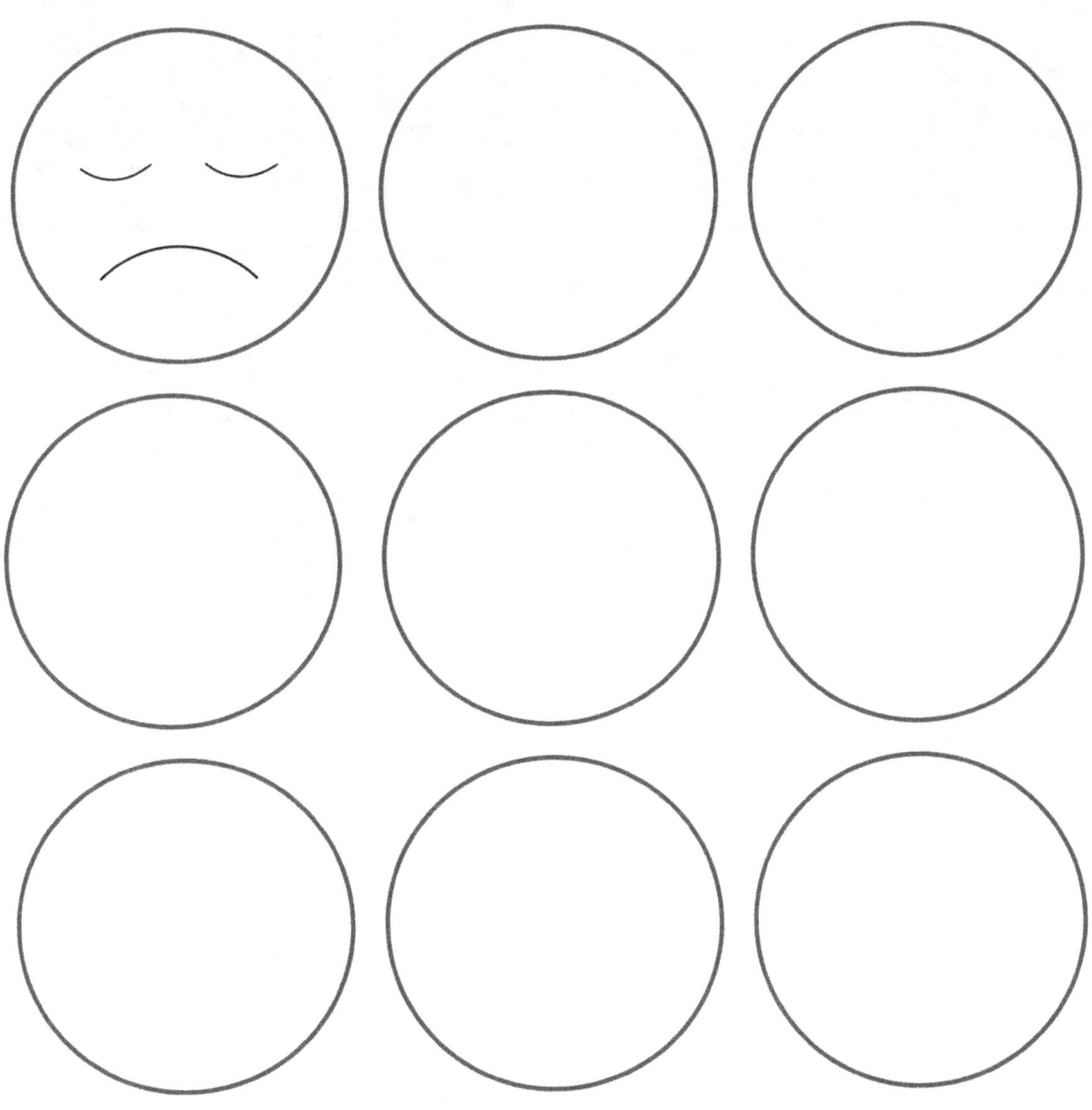

Us, Together

Describe or draw your favorite things that you used to do together with your loved one.

Feel Good Things
- PART 2 -

What are your favorite fun activities?

What are your favorite relaxing activities?

Gold Stars

Write out some of your achievements in the stars and color them in.

Accomplishments

It is important to celebrate our ability to do things that are challenging. What is something you have accomplished that was hard to do?

_____

_____

_____

_____

_____

_____

Fill Your Cup

Draw symbols that remind you of your loved one in the cup.

What do these symbols represent?

_____

_____

_____

Musical Connection

Does music help you feel connected to your loved one?

Yes	No

List out some of your favorite songs
that make you feel good:

Write Them A Letter
- Part 2 -

Guess what! You wouldn't believe that:

I want you to know that:

Word Search

- PART 2 -

```
D C U Z N S J B M I E G E Q W
D N O T F L I E K C H N B A D
C G E M E Z M F A E G I P H U
N Q A I F O T E A V R S M E C
V B M W R O P R U O I S O Z R
B L W Y N F R J A L E I J E Z
T H E R A P Y T S E F M B F L
C S G N I L E E F F H M Q T P
P I H S N O I T A L E R B M W
H N F C B H V O A M T X E G X
J G G J N K V S Z E F L M E S U
V Q K N M S G R V V X V A L U
```

COMFORT	RELATIONSHIP	REMEMBER	THERAPY
GRIEF	HEART	FRIEND	LOVE
MEMORY	MISSING	PEACE	FEELINGS

The Roller Coaster

Some people describe grief as a roller coaster because it is like a journey with twists and turns.

What moments have felt tough to experience?

_____

_____

_____

What moments have felt good to experience?

_____

_____

_____

Mementos

Do you have keepsakes that remind you of your loved one? Describe or draw the objects you keep.

Would You Rather

- PART 3 -

Color in what you like best.

Share memories with others

or

Think about memories by yourself

Keep your feelings private

or

Share how you feel with others

Talk about them in the past tense

or

Talk about them in the present tense

Fill your day with many activities

or

Have more free time in your day

Message In A Bottle

If you could send out a message in a bottle for your loved one, what would you want to write in your note?

_____

_____

_____

_____

_____

_____

_____

_____

A-maze-ing Friends

Find your way through the maze to meet
up with your friends.

Journal & Memory Pages

_____

_____

_____

_____

_____

_____

_____

_____

_____

_____

Share Your Completed Pages With Us

Share On Your Pages

We invite you to join our community on Instagram: **@snapshotsoflifeafterloss**

Tag us when you post your completed pages - we would love to see them!

Share On Our Pages

Use the QR code to upload your completed pages to our website and social media pages.

About Our Foundation

Luna Peak Foundation is a 501(c)(3) nonprofit organization. We support cancer fighters and grief survivors by providing unique resources to help them survive the hardships of a cancer diagnosis or losing a loved one. We elevate multicultural survivor stories and use photography, books, and workshops to show people that they are not alone. Our books aim to inspire, spread hope, and give back to the community. Luna Peak has donated thousands of books to hospitals, support groups, schools, and therapist offices.

100% of book sales benefit Luna Peak Foundation.
Thank you for buying this book and paying it forward.

Join our mission - www.lunapeakfoundation.org
Shop our books - www.lunapeakpublishing.com/shop

Other Books By Luna Peak:

Many titles are available in Spanish

The Grief Workbook
The Pet Loss Grief Workbook
Beyond Grief: Snapshots of Life After Loss
Season's Griefings: A Holiday Grief Workbook
Beyond Remission: Words of Advice for Thriving
My History of the Covid Pandemic: A Journal for Kids
Kicking Cancer: A Memory Book for Kids
Sean's Best Week at Camp Luna Peak
Follow Me, Cancer Free
Color Me, Cancer Free